DAILY SELF-CARE AFFIRMATIONS FOR BUSY BLACK WOMEN

CULTIVATING SELF-CARE HABITS; EMPOWERING PRACTICES FOR A HEALTHY MIND, BODY, AND SOUL

MICHELLE WOODS

Copyright © 2023 by Michelle Woods. All rights reserved.

The content within this book may not be reproduced, duplicated, or transmitted without direct written permission from the author or the publisher.

Under no circumstances will any blame or legal responsibility be held against the publisher, or author, for any damages, reparation, or monetary loss due to the information contained within this book, either directly or indirectly.

Legal Notice:

This book is copyright protected. It is only for personal use. You cannot amend, distribute, sell, use, quote, or paraphrase any part of the content within this book, without the consent of the author or publisher.

Disclaimer Notice:

Please note the information contained within this document is for educational and entertainment purposes only. All effort has been expended to present accurate, up-to-date, reliable, and complete information. No warranties of any kind are declared or implied. Readers acknowledge that the author is not engaged in the rendering of legal, financial, medical, or professional advice. The content within this book has been derived from various sources. Please consult a licensed professional before attempting any techniques outlined in this book.

By reading this document, the reader agrees that under no circumstances is the author responsible for any losses, direct or indirect, that are incurred as a result of the use of the information contained within this document, including, but not limited to, errors, omissions, or inaccuracies.

CONTENTS

Introduction   5

1. UNDERSTANDING SELF-CARE   9
   Defining Self-Care   11
   The Power of Daily Affirmations   11
   Conclusion   13

2. THE POWER OF DAILY AFFIRMATIONS   15
   The Science Behind Affirmations   17
   Benefits of Daily Affirmations   19
   Examples of Affirmations   20
   Conclusion   21

3. MINDFULNESS AND PRESENCE   23
   Introduction   24
   Section 1: Understanding Mindfulness   25
   Section 2: Daily Affirmations for Mindfulness   29
   Section 3: Practical Exercises and Techniques   34
   Conclusion   41

4. STRESS RELIEF AND RELAXATION   45

5. NURTURING HEALTHY HABITS: EMBRACING A BALANCED AND VIBRANT LIFE   53
   Section 1: The Significance of Healthy Habits   54
   Section 2: Affirmations for Healthy Eating   56
   Section 3: Affirmations for Exercise and Movement   57

Section 4: Affirmations for Restful Sleep	59
Section 5: Affirmations for Self-Care Routines	61
6. CULTIVATING POSITIVE THINKING	65
7. SELF-CARE BEYOND THE DAILY AFFIRMATIONS	73
Section 1: The Power of Self-Reflection	75
Section 2: Cultivating Self-Compassion	78
Section 3: Seeking Support and Connection	81
Section 4: Exploring Self-Care Resources	84
Conclusion: Embracing the Power of Self-Care	89
Summary	95
Image Resources	117

INTRODUCTION

> "I am an example of what is possible when girls from the very beginning of their lives are loved and nurtured by people around them. I was surrounded by extraordinary women in my life who taught me about quiet strength and dignity."
>
> — MICHELLE OBAMA

In a fast-paced world that often demands our constant attention and energy, it is crucial for busy Black women to prioritize self-care. We are mothers, daughters, sisters, and professionals juggling multiple responsibilities and navigating various challenges. We are the backbone of our communities, always giving our all to support others. But amid our busy lives, we often neglect to take care of ourselves.

Self-care is not a luxury but a necessity for our overall well-being. It is an act of self-love and empowerment, allowing us to recharge, rejuvenate, and show up fully in every aspect of our lives. It is about nurturing our minds, bodies, and souls, and creating a harmonious balance that sustains us in our journey.

That is why I am thrilled to present *Daily Self-Care Affirmations for Busy Black Women: Cultivating Self-Care Habits; Empowering Practices for a Healthy Mind, Body, and Soul.* This book is a compassionate guide, designed specifically for Black women who are seeking practical and meaningful ways to prioritize self-care in their daily lives. It offers a collection of powerful affirmations that will inspire, uplift, and support us on our path to wellness.

The purpose of this book is twofold. First, it aims to remind us of the importance of self-care and provide gentle reminders to prioritize our well-being amid our busy schedules. Through the affirmations, we are encouraged to carve out moments of self-reflection, acknowledge our worth, and set boundaries that protect our energy and preserve our mental and emotional health.

Secondly, this book serves as a practical tool to guide us in implementing simple self-care practices. Each affirmation is carefully crafted to address specific areas of our lives, such as mindfulness, stress relief, healthy habits, and positive thinking. By incorporating these affirmations into our daily routine, we are creating a sacred space for self-care, where we can find solace, strength, and renewal.

My hope is that this book becomes a companion, a source of inspiration, and a gentle reminder that self-care is not a selfish act but an act of self-preservation. As busy Black women, we must learn to nurture ourselves so that we can continue to uplift and support others. Through these daily affirmations, we can cultivate a deep sense of self-love, reclaim our power, and thrive in every aspect of our lives.

I invite you to embark on this transformative journey of self-care with me. Let us embrace the power of daily affirmations and the profound impact they can have on our well-being. Together, let us create a culture of self-care within our community, where every busy Black woman feels empowered, loved, and nourished.

Thank you for choosing *Daily Self-Care Affirmations for Busy Black Women: Cultivating Self-Care Habits; Empowering Practices for a Healthy Mind, Body, and Soul.* May it serve as a gentle reminder to prioritize your self-care, embrace your worth, and live a life filled with love, joy, and well-being.

UNDERSTANDING SELF-CARE

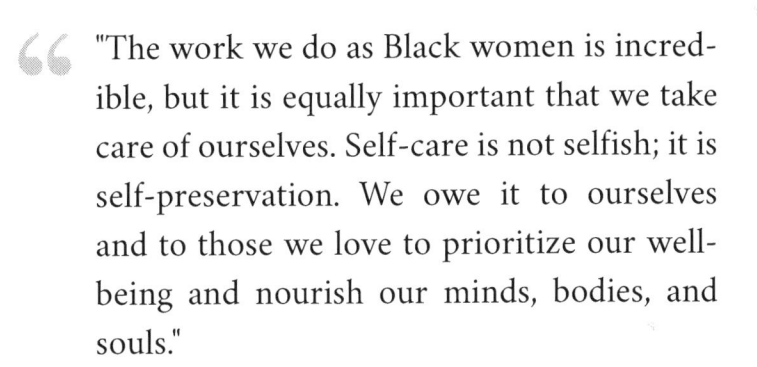

> "The work we do as Black women is incredible, but it is equally important that we take care of ourselves. Self-care is not selfish; it is self-preservation. We owe it to ourselves and to those we love to prioritize our well-being and nourish our minds, bodies, and souls."
>
> — MICHELLE OBAMA

In a world that constantly demands our attention and energy, self-care has become more important than ever. As busy Black women, we often find ourselves juggling multiple roles and responsibilities, putting the needs of others before our own. We are the backbone of our families, communities, and workplaces, constantly striving to excel in every aspect of our lives. But in the process, we often neglect our own well-being, pushing aside our needs and desires in the pursuit of success and fulfillment.

In this chapter, we will delve into the concept of self-care and its significance in maintaining our overall well-being. We will explore the unique challenges faced by busy Back women in prioritizing self-care, and we will introduce the powerful tool of daily affirmations as a means of nurturing and nourishing our minds, bodies, and souls.

DEFINING SELF-CARE

Self-care is more than just indulging in occasional pampering or relaxation. It is a holistic practice that encompasses caring for our physical, mental, and emotional well-being. It is a deliberate and intentional act of showing love and compassion to ourselves, acknowledging that we are worthy of care and attention. Self-care is about nurturing our bodies, tending to our minds, and honoring our souls.

As busy Black women, we face unique challenges in prioritizing self-care. Our lives are often filled with a constant stream of responsibilities and obligations. We are expected to be strong, resilient, and capable in every aspect of our lives. But amid all our busyness, we must remember that we cannot pour from an empty cup. We must take the time to replenish ourselves, recharge our spirits, and care for our own well-being.

THE POWER OF DAILY AFFIRMATIONS

One powerful tool that can support us on our self-care journey is the practice of daily affirmations. Affirmations are positive statements that we repeat to ourselves, consciously and intentionally, to reinforce positive beliefs and thoughts. They serve as reminders of our worth, our strengths, and our capabilities. Affirmations have the power to shift our mindset, reframe our perspectives, and cultivate a more positive and empowering inner dialogue.

Daily affirmations offer us a consistent and reliable practice to anchor ourselves in self-care. They provide a moment of pause amid the chaos in our lives, allowing us to tune into our inner selves and reconnect with our deepest desires and needs. By incorporating daily affirmations into our routines, we create a sacred space for self-reflection, self-compassion, and self-empowerment.

In this book, we have curated a collection of daily affirmations specifically designed for busy Black women. These affirmations address the unique challenges we face and speak directly to our experiences, dreams, and aspirations. They cover a range of topics, including mindfulness, stress relief, healthy habits, and positive thinking. Each affirmation is crafted with intention and love, with the sole purpose of supporting and empowering us on our self-care journey.

CONCLUSION

As busy Black women, it is crucial that we prioritize self-care. It is not a luxury reserved for the privileged few, but a necessity for our overall well-being. Self-care is an act of self-preservation, a radical act of love and resistance. By taking the time to care for ourselves, we are not only honoring our own worth but also setting an example for future generations of Black women.

In the chapters that follow, we will dive deeper into the various aspects of self-care, exploring practical strategies and techniques to integrate self-care into our daily lives. Through the power of daily affirmations, we will embark on a transformative journey of self-discovery, self-love, and self-empowerment. Together, we will reclaim our right to care for ourselves and create a life filled with joy, fulfillment, and well-being.

Thank you for joining me on this journey of self-care. May this book serve as a guiding light, a source of inspiration, and a gentle reminder that you are worthy of love, care, and nourishment. Let us embark on this empowering challenge together, knowing that we have the strength and resilience to thrive as busy Black women.

2

THE POWER OF DAILY AFFIRMATIONS

> *"I believe in the power of affirmations to shape our mindset and transform our lives. By incorporating daily affirmations into our self-care routine, we can nurture a positive and empowering inner dialogue that propels us towards personal growth and well-being."*
>
> — KAMALA HARRIS

In this chapter, we delve into the transformative power of daily affirmations and their profound impact on our mindset, well-being, and overall sense of self. As busy Black women, it is essential that we embrace the power of positive self-talk and cultivate a mindset that uplifts and empowers us. Through the simple practice of daily affirmations, we can harness the strength within us and navigate life's challenges with resilience and grace.

In addition, we explore various techniques and strategies to integrate daily affirmations seamlessly into our busy lives. We understand that time is a precious commodity, and finding moments for self-reflection and positive affirmations may seem challenging. However, we provide practical tips and guidance to make the practice of daily affirmations a seamless part of our routine. Whether it's incorporating affirmations into our morning rituals, using technology to set reminders throughout the day, or finding pockets of stillness in our hectic schedules, we discover ways to prioritize self-care and affirm our worth consistently. By committing to the practice of daily affirmations, we create a foundation of strength, resilience, and self-love that empowers us to navigate the world with unwavering confidence and embrace our unique journey as busy Black women.

THE SCIENCE BEHIND AFFIRMATIONS

Affirmations are not just mere words; they carry the potential to rewire our brains and shape our beliefs and actions. Scientific research has shown that the brain responds to positive affirmations by releasing feel-good neurotransmitters, such as dopamine and serotonin, which enhance our mood and overall well-being. Furthermore, affirmations have been found to activate regions in the brain associated with self-valuation and self-regulation, leading to improved self-esteem and self-confidence.

When we repeat affirmations, we are essentially rewiring our thought patterns and replacing negative self-talk with empowering and uplifting messages. This process is rooted in the concept of neuroplasticity, the brain's ability to form new neural connections and change its structure in response to our thoughts and experiences. By consistently practicing affirmations, we can create new neural pathways that support positive beliefs and attitudes.

The power of affirmations extends beyond our thoughts and influences our actions as well. When we believe in ourselves and our capabilities, we are more likely to take action, set goals, and persevere in the face of challenges. Affirmations can fuel our motivation, instill a sense of purpose, and inspire us to take the necessary steps toward our aspirations.

Moreover, affirmations have been found to have a profound impact on our emotional well-being. They can help reduce stress, anxiety, and self-doubt, allowing us to cultivate a more positive and resilient mindset. Affirmations promote self-compassion, reminding us to be kind and gentle with ourselves, especially during times of difficulty. They serve as powerful tools for building resilience and bouncing back from setbacks, reinforcing the belief that we are capable of overcoming obstacles and achieving success.

Research has also highlighted the social and interpersonal benefits of affirmations. When we affirm ourselves positively, we radiate confidence and attract positive energy, which can enhance our relationships and interactions with others. Affirmations can foster a sense of empathy and compassion toward ourselves and those around us, creating a more harmonious and supportive social environment.

In essence, the science behind affirmations validates their transformative power in shaping our thoughts, beliefs, and actions. By incorporating affirmations into our daily lives, we tap into the incredible potential of our minds to create positive change and cultivate a mindset of self-love, confidence, and empowerment. As we embrace the science behind affirmations, let us embrace the journey of personal growth and harness the limitless possibilities that lie within us.

BENEFITS OF DAILY AFFIRMATIONS

Incorporating daily affirmations into our self-care routine can yield numerous benefits for our mental, emotional, and even physical health. By consciously choosing positive and empowering statements, we create a fertile ground for self-growth and personal development. Daily affirmations help us challenge negative self-talk, overcome self-doubt, and cultivate a mindset of abundance and possibility.

Affirmations can have a profound impact on our emotional well-being. They serve as a powerful antidote to stress, anxiety, and self-limiting beliefs. By repeating affirmations that resonate with us, we invite positive emotions, such as joy, gratitude, and resilience, into our lives. This emotional shift allows us to approach challenges with a renewed sense of confidence and determination.

EXAMPLES OF AFFIRMATIONS

To fully embrace the power of daily affirmations, it is important to find statements that deeply resonate with our personal experiences and aspirations. Here are some examples of affirmations specifically tailored for busy Black women:

1. "I am deserving of rest, rejuvenation, and self-care."
2. "I embrace my strength, resilience, and ability to overcome any obstacle."
3. "I am worthy of love, joy, and success in all areas of my life."
4. "I honor my boundaries and prioritize my well-being."
5. "I release any negative self-talk and embrace the power of positive thinking."

6. "I am capable, confident, and ready to pursue my dreams."
7. "I am enough, just as I am, and I celebrate my unique gifts and talents."
8. "I radiate beauty, grace, and self-assurance."
9. "I am the architect of my own happiness and success."
10. "I attract abundance, prosperity, and opportunities into my life."

These affirmations serve as empowering reminders of our worth, strength, and resilience. By incorporating them into our daily routine, we can transform our inner dialogue and cultivate a mindset of self-love, confidence, and limitless potential.

CONCLUSION

Chapter 2 sets the stage for our journey of self-discovery and empowerment through the practice of daily affirmations. We have explored the science behind affirmations and witnessed their profound impact on mindset and well-being. Now, armed with the knowledge and understanding of the power of positive self-talk, we are ready to embrace daily affirmations as a transformative tool for self-care and personal growth. Together, let us affirm our worth, celebrate our strengths, and unleash our fullest potential as busy Black women on the path to holistic well-being.

MINDFULNESS AND PRESENCE

> *"Mindfulness is the key to unlocking the fullness of life. It allows us to awaken to the present moment and embrace it with a deep sense of gratitude and wonder. Through mindfulness, we can find peace in the midst of chaos and cultivate a profound connection to ourselves and the world around us."*
>
> — OPRAH WINFREY

INTRODUCTION

In today's fast-paced world, it can be challenging for busy Black women to find moments of calm and stillness. The demands of work, family, and personal responsibilities can leave little time for self-care and reflection. However, it is precisely during these busy moments that the practice of mindfulness becomes even more essential. In this chapter, we will delve into the transformative power of mindfulness and how it can enhance the well-being of busy Black women. We will explore the benefits of mindfulness, introduce daily affirmations that promote mindfulness and presence, and provide practical exercises and techniques to incorporate mindfulness into daily life.

Moreover, we will address the unique challenges faced by busy Black women in prioritizing self-care and mindfulness. We recognize the external pressures and societal expectations that often burden us, making it even more crucial to carve out time for ourselves. Through the practice of mindfulness and the daily affirmations tailored specifically for busy Black women, we empower ourselves to reclaim our moments of stillness, center ourselves in the present, and nurture our inner peace. By embracing mindfulness as a powerful tool, we not only cultivate a deeper connection with ourselves but also cultivate a sense of resilience and strength that allows us to navigate the complexities of life with grace and authenticity. Let us embark on this journey together, unlocking the transformative power of mindfulness and embracing the power within us as busy Black women.

SECTION 1: UNDERSTANDING MINDFULNESS

1.1 Defining Mindfulness

Mindfulness is the practice of being fully present in the moment, without judgment or attachment to thoughts and emotions. It involves paying attention to our thoughts, feelings, and sensations with curiosity and acceptance. By cultivating mindfulness, we can develop a deeper awareness of ourselves and the world around us.

Mindfulness is not just a state of mind, but a way of being. It invites us to slow down and tune in to the present moment, allowing us to fully experience and appreciate life as it unfolds. It is a powerful tool that helps us break free from the autopilot mode of living and connect with our inner selves. In a world that often demands constant multitasking and distraction, mindfulness offers a refuge—a space where we can find solace, clarity, and a renewed sense of purpose.

When we practice mindfulness, we become observers of our thoughts, emotions, and bodily sensations. We learn to witness them without judgment or the need to change them. This nonjudgmental awareness allows us to cultivate self-compassion and embrace ourselves exactly as we are in each moment. It teaches us to let go of the past and future, and to anchor ourselves in the present, where true peace and contentment reside.

By incorporating mindfulness into our daily lives, we can begin to break free from the cycle of stress, anxiety, and overwhelm. We gain the ability to respond to life's challenges with greater clarity and resilience. Mindfulness empowers us to pause, take a breath, and make intentional choices rather than react impulsively. It helps us develop emotional intelligence, improve our relationships, and foster a deeper connection to ourselves and others.

As busy Black women, the practice of mindfulness becomes even more essential. We often juggle multiple roles and responsibilities, navigate societal pressures, and face unique challenges. Mindfulness provides us with a sanctuary—a safe haven where we can replenish our spirits, restore our energy, and reclaim our inner peace. It reminds us to prioritize our well-being and honor our own needs, allowing us to show up fully and authentically in every aspect of our lives.

Throughout this chapter, we will delve deeper into the concept of mindfulness and explore various practices that can help us cultivate this state of presence and awareness. From breath-focused exercises to body scans, we will discover the tools that resonate with us individually. Let us embark on this transformative journey together, embracing the power of mindfulness to nourish our minds, bodies, and souls.

1.2 Benefits of Mindfulness

Research has shown that practicing mindfulness can have numerous benefits for mental, emotional, and physical well-being. It can reduce stress, anxiety, and depression, improve focus and concentration, enhance self-awareness and emotional regulation, and promote overall resilience and inner peace. For busy Black women, these benefits are especially valuable in navigating the challenges and pressures they may face.

In a world that often demands constant productivity and achievement, mindfulness offers a counterbalance —a gentle reminder to slow down, take a breath, and reconnect with ourselves. By cultivating mindfulness, we create space to pause and respond to life's challenges with intention and clarity. We become more attuned to our own needs, allowing us to establish healthy boundaries and make choices that align with our values and priorities.

For busy Black women, the benefits of mindfulness extend beyond individual well-being. Mindfulness empowers us to navigate the intersections of our identities and embrace the fullness of who we are. It provides a foundation for self-compassion, self-acceptance, and self-love, allowing us to embrace our unique experiences, strengths, and resilience. Through mindfulness, we can transcend societal expectations and limitations, and redefine success and fulfillment on our own terms.

In addition to its individual benefits, mindfulness also has the power to ripple outward and positively impact our relationships and communities. When we cultivate mindfulness, we develop greater empathy, compassion, and understanding toward others. We become more present and attentive listeners, creating space for authentic connection and meaningful conversations. As we embody mindfulness in our interactions, we inspire those around us to do the same, fostering a culture of well-being and collective growth.

Throughout this chapter, we will explore the multifaceted benefits of mindfulness in more depth. We will delve into the research and scientific evidence supporting its effectiveness, and we will share personal stories of how mindfulness has transformed the lives of busy Black women. Together, we will embrace the power of mindfulness and unlock its profound potential to cultivate a healthier mind, body, and soul. Let us embark on this journey of self-discovery and empowerment, as we discover the transformative impact of mindfulness in our lives.

SECTION 2: DAILY AFFIRMATIONS FOR MINDFULNESS

2.1 The Power of Daily Affirmations

Daily affirmations are positive statements that we repeat to ourselves to reinforce positive beliefs and attitudes. When it comes to mindfulness, affirmations can help anchor our attention to the present moment, cultivate a sense of gratitude and acceptance, and foster a compassionate and nonjudgmental attitude toward ourselves and others.

The power of daily affirmations lies in their ability to shape our thoughts, emotions, and actions. By intentionally choosing positive and empowering statements, we create a mental landscape that is conducive to growth, self-love, and resilience. Affirmations serve as gentle reminders of our inherent worth, potential, and capacity for greatness.

When we incorporate affirmations into our mindfulness practice, we invite a deeper sense of presence and awareness. Affirmations act as guiding lights, directing our attention to the present moment and anchoring us in the here and now. As we repeat affirmations, we cultivate a conscious connection with our thoughts, feelings, and sensations, fostering a greater sense of self-awareness and clarity.

Moreover, affirmations can help us cultivate a mindset of gratitude and acceptance. By affirming the positive aspects of ourselves and our lives, we shift our focus away from negativity and embrace a perspective of abundance. Affirmations encourage us to recognize and appreciate the blessings, opportunities, and strengths that surround us. Through this practice, we develop a sense of gratitude that permeates our entire being, uplifting our spirits and nurturing a deep sense of contentment.

Affirmations also foster a compassionate and nonjudgmental attitude toward ourselves and others. As we repeat affirmations that promote self-love and self-acceptance, we counteract negative self-talk and self-criticism. We learn to treat ourselves with kindness, patience, and understanding, acknowledging that we are worthy of love and respect. This compassionate inner dialogue extends beyond ourselves and shapes the way we interact with others. Through affirmations, we cultivate empathy, compassion, and acceptance, nurturing healthier and more fulfilling relationships.

Incorporating daily affirmations into our mindfulness practice is an invitation to be intentional and deliberate in our self-care journey. It is an opportunity to consciously shape our inner dialogue and beliefs, creating a positive and empowering foundation for our thoughts, emotions, and actions. By embracing the power of daily affirmations, we take an active role in shaping our reality and nurturing a mindset that supports our well-being and personal growth.

Throughout this chapter, we will explore different techniques and strategies for incorporating daily affirmations into our mindfulness practice. We will provide a diverse range of affirmations that cater specifically to the needs and experiences of busy Black women. Together, we will harness the transformative power of affirmations and unlock the potential for self-love, confidence, and empowerment that lies within each of us. Let us embark on this journey of self-discovery and affirmation, as we create a foundation of positivity and resilience in our lives.

2.2 Affirmations for Mindfulness and Presence

In this section, we will introduce a collection of daily affirmations specifically curated to promote mindfulness and presence in the lives of busy Black women. These affirmations will encourage cultivating mindfulness in everyday activities, such as during self-care routines, work tasks, and interactions with loved ones. They will serve as gentle reminders to slow down, be fully present, and embrace the beauty and richness of each moment.

1. I am fully present in this moment, embracing the beauty and abundance it offers.
2. My breath anchors me to the present, allowing me to experience each moment with clarity and calmness.

3. I release thoughts of the past and worries about the future, choosing to be fully present in the here and now.
4. I engage in my daily activities with mindful awareness, savoring every sensation and finding joy in the simplest moments.
5. Each breath I take nourishes my mind, body, and soul, reminding me of the precious gift of life.
6. I embrace silence and stillness, allowing myself to be fully present and open to the wisdom within.
7. I let go of distractions and focus my attention on the task at hand, immersing myself in the present moment.
8. I approach each interaction with love, compassion, and mindfulness, fostering deeper connections and understanding.
9. I choose to be an observer of my thoughts and emotions, acknowledging them without judgment, and letting them pass.
10. I cultivate gratitude for the present moment, recognizing that it is a gift that holds infinite possibilities.

These affirmations are designed to support busy Black women in cultivating mindfulness and presence in their daily lives. By incorporating them into your mindfulness practice, you can enhance your ability to be fully present, embrace the present moment, and experience greater peace and fulfillment.

SECTION 3: PRACTICAL EXERCISES AND TECHNIQUES

3.1 Breathing Exercises

One of the fundamental aspects of mindfulness is focusing on the breath. We will explore various breathing exercises that can be incorporated into daily life to bring about a sense of calm and centeredness. These exercises will help ground busy Black women in the present moment and provide a respite from the busyness of life.

1. **Deep Belly Breathing:** Sit or lie down in a comfortable position. Place one hand on your belly and the other hand on your chest. Take a slow, deep breath in through your nose, allowing your belly to rise as you fill your lungs with air. Exhale slowly through your mouth, feeling your belly sink back down. Repeat this deep belly breathing for several breaths,

focusing on the sensation of your breath entering and leaving your body.

2. **Box Breathing:** Visualize a box shape in your mind. Inhale deeply for a count of four as you trace the first side of the box in your mind. Hold your breath for a count of four as you trace the second side of the box. Exhale slowly for a count of four as you trace the third side of the box. Hold your breath again for a count of four as you trace the fourth side of the box. Repeat this box breathing pattern for several rounds, allowing yourself to find a rhythm and focus on the box visualization.

3. **4–7–8 Breathing:** Start by exhaling completely through your mouth, making a whooshing sound. Close your mouth and inhale quietly through your nose to a mental count of four. Hold your breath for a count of seven. Exhale completely through your mouth to a count of eight, again making a whooshing sound. Repeat this 4–7–8 breathing pattern for several cycles, feeling a sense of relaxation and release with each exhale.

Remember, these are just a few examples of breathing exercises that can be practiced for mindfulness and relaxation. Feel free to explore different techniques and find what works best for you. The key is to focus your attention on your breath, allowing it to anchor you to the present moment and bring a sense of calm and centeredness to your busy life.

3.2 *Mindful Movement*

Engaging in mindful movement practices, such as yoga or tai chi, can help connect the mind and body, promoting a deeper sense of awareness and presence. We will discuss different forms of mindful movements and provide guidance on incorporating them into daily routines.

1. **Yoga:** Yoga is a practice that combines physical postures, breath control, and meditation. It

promotes strength, flexibility, and mindfulness. Try incorporating a short yoga routine into your daily self-care practice. Focus on moving slowly and deliberately, paying attention to each movement and sensation in your body. Engage in poses that promote balance, strength, and relaxation, such as the Mountain Pose, Tree Pose, and Child's Pose. Allow yourself to fully immerse in the practice, bringing your attention to the present moment and cultivating a sense of calm and awareness.

2. **Tai Chi:** Tai chi is a gentle martial art that emphasizes slow, flowing movements and deep breathing. It is known for its ability to promote relaxation, balance, and mental clarity. Consider incorporating a few minutes of tai chi into your daily routine. Practice slow, deliberate movements, paying attention to the sensations in your body and the flow of energy. - Focus on maintaining a calm and steady breath, syncing your movements with your inhalations and exhalations. Allow yourself to experience the meditative qualities of tai chi as you move with intention and grace.

3. **Walking Meditation:** Walking can be transformed into a mindful movement practice by incorporating mindfulness techniques. Find

a quiet outdoor space where you can take a leisurely walk without distractions. As you walk, bring your attention to the sensations in your body—the feeling of your feet connecting with the ground, the movement of your legs, and the rhythm of your breath. Notice the sights, sounds, and smells around you without judgment. If your mind wanders, gently bring your focus back to the present moment and the physical sensations of walking. This practice can help you cultivate a sense of grounding, peace, and connection with your body and the environment.

Remember, these are just a few examples of mindful movement practices. Feel free to explore other activities that resonate with you, such as dance, qigong, or hiking. The key is to engage in movement with a heightened sense of awareness, allowing yourself to fully experience the present moment and nourish your mind, body, and soul.

3.3 Gratitude and Reflection

Practicing gratitude and reflection is an integral part of mindfulness. We will explore techniques for cultivating gratitude and creating a reflective practice that allows busy Black women to pause, appreciate their achievements, and find meaning and purpose in their daily lives.

1. **Gratitude Journaling:** Set aside a few minutes each day to write down things you are grateful for. Reflect on the positive aspects of your life, big or small, and express your gratitude through words. Write down three things you are grateful for that happened during the day or reflect on moments, experiences, or people that brought you joy or made a positive impact on your life. This practice helps shift your focus to the blessings and abundance in your life, fostering a sense of appreciation and contentment.
2. **Mindful Appreciation:** Take a moment each day to consciously appreciate the present moment. Pause and observe your surroundings, noticing the beauty and details that often go unnoticed. It could be the warmth of the sunlight, the sound of birds chirping, or the aroma of your morning coffee. Engage your senses fully and allow yourself to be fully present in the moment, cultivating a sense of gratitude for the simple joys of life.

3. **Reflection Time:** Create dedicated time for reflection and introspection. Set aside a specific time each day, whether it's in the morning or before bed, to sit in quiet contemplation. Use this time to reflect on your experiences, emotions, and thoughts. Ask yourself questions such as "What am I proud of today?" or "What lessons did I learn?" Reflect on your successes, challenges, and areas for growth. This practice allows you to gain insight into yourself, develop self-awareness, and find meaning and purpose in your daily life.

4. **Gratitude Rituals:** Incorporate gratitude into your daily rituals or routines. For example, before a meal, take a moment to express gratitude for the food on your plate and the nourishment it provides. Before bed, reflect on three things you are grateful for from the day. By infusing gratitude into your daily rituals, you create a habit of acknowledging the blessings in your life and cultivate a positive mindset.

Remember, practicing gratitude and reflection is a personal journey. Find the techniques that resonate with you and make them a part of your daily self-care routine. The more you cultivate gratitude and reflection, the more you will nurture a positive and appreciative mindset, leading to greater fulfillment and joy in your life.

CONCLUSION

In this chapter, we have explored the power of mindfulness and presence in the lives of busy Black women. We have discussed the benefits of mindfulness, introduced daily affirmations that promote mindfulness and presence, and provided practical exercises and techniques to incorporate mindfulness into daily life. By cultivating mindfulness, we can find moments of peace and clarity amid the chaos, enhance our well-being, and deepen our connection to ourselves and the world around us. Through the practice of mindfulness and the use of affirmations, busy Black women can navigate their lives with greater presence, resilience, and inner peace.

EMPOWER BLACK WOMEN TO THRIVE AND EMBRACE SELF-LOVE

"Success is liking yourself, liking what you do, and liking how you do it."

— MAYA ANGELOU

By leaving a review of "Daily Self-Care Affirmations for Busy Black Women: Cultivating Self-Care Habits; Empowering Practices for a Healthy Mind, Body and Soul" on Amazon, you can play a pivotal role in guiding other women towards the transformative power of affirmations. Your honest feedback will assist them in navigating their personal journeys and discovering the self-love, confidence, and empowerment they deserve.

Share Your Insights:

Your review holds the key to unlocking the potential within other Black women who are seeking guidance, inspiration, and tools to cultivate self-love and embrace their true worth. By sharing your thoughts and experiences, you can provide valuable insights that will help them embark on their own transformative path.

Guide Women Towards Empowerment:

Every word of your review is an opportunity to empower and uplift other Black women. Help them discover the strength and resilience that lie within by expressing how this book has positively impacted your own journey. Your words will guide them towards a deeper sense of self-love, confidence, and empowerment.

Illuminate the Path:

Your review acts as a guiding light amidst the challenges and uncertainties many Black women face. By sharing the ways in which this book has illuminated your path and provided clarity, you offer a beacon of hope to others who are searching for direction and inspiration.

Inspire Confidence:

Your honest feedback can inspire a sense of confidence in potential readers, assuring them that "Daily Self-Care Affirmations for Busy Black Women" is a powerful resource that can positively impact their lives. Your words have the potential to uplift and motivate them to take the next step towards self-love and personal growth.

Make a Difference:

Your voice has the power to make a lasting difference in the lives of Black women. By leaving a review on Amazon, you actively contribute to building a community of empowered individuals who are united in their pursuit of self-love, confidence, and empowerment. Together, we can create a supportive network that uplifts and inspires.

Your review is a gift that keeps on giving, as it empowers and supports other Black women on their path to self-discovery and personal growth. Together, let's create a community where every Black woman feels empowered, confident, and inspired to embrace their authentic selves.

Scan the QR code below for a quick review!

4

STRESS RELIEF AND RELAXATION

"Finding inner peace amidst the chaos is a radical act of self-love. Prioritizing stress relief and relaxation allows us to recharge our spirits, restore balance, and conquer any challenge that comes our way. Remember, you have the power to create a sanctuary of tranquility within yourself, no matter how busy life may be."

— SERENA WILLIAMS

In the fast-paced world we live in, stress has become an all-too-familiar companion. As busy Black women juggling multiple responsibilities, the pressure can be even more overwhelming. It is crucial to recognize the importance of managing stress and finding moments of relaxation to protect our well-being and maintain a sense of balance.

Stress affects us on multiple levels—mentally, emotionally, and physically. It can hinder our ability to perform at our best, impact our relationships, and even undermine our health. That is why it is essential to prioritize stress relief and develop strategies to unwind and recharge.

In this chapter, we invite you to embark on a journey of self-discovery and reflection as we delve into the topic of stress relief and relaxation. We recognize the unique challenges faced by busy Black women and the immense pressures that can weigh us down. It is crucial to understand why making time for self-care practices that promote a sense of calm and rejuvenation is not just a luxury but a necessity for our overall well-being.

As busy Black women, we often find ourselves caught up in a never-ending cycle of responsibilities, obligations, and expectations. We give so much of ourselves to others that we often forget to prioritize our own needs. We may neglect self-care, believing that taking time for ourselves is selfish or indulgent. However, it is essential to recognize that self-care is not a luxury; it is a fundamental aspect of maintaining our physical, mental, and emotional health.

Stress management is not about seeking temporary relief from the pressures of life; it is about adopting healthy coping mechanisms that support our overall well-being. It is about recognizing the signs of stress and taking proactive steps to address them before they escalate. It is about cultivating resilience and finding balance amid life's never-ending demands.

By making time for self-care practices, we create an opportunity to recharge, rejuvenate, and replenish our energy reserves. It is not a selfish act; it is an act of self-preservation. When we prioritize our well-being, we are better equipped to navigate the challenges that come our way. We become more resilient, more focused, and more capable of fulfilling our various roles and responsibilities.

Throughout this chapter, we will explore a range of self-care practices that can help promote stress relief and relaxation. We will delve into the power of mindfulness, the benefits of physical activity, the importance of sleep and rest, and the impact of nourishing our bodies with healthy nutrition. We will also discuss the significance of setting boundaries, practicing self-compassion, and seeking support from our communities.

So, as we embark on this exploration of stress relief and relaxation, let us remember that self-care is not a luxury, but a vital aspect of our well-being. Let us embrace the notion that by taking care of ourselves, we are better able to care for others. By adopting healthy coping mechanisms, we not only enhance our own lives but also inspire those around us to prioritize their well-being.

Together, let us challenge the notion that stress and overwhelm are inevitable parts of our lives as busy Black women. Let us rewrite the narrative and create a culture of self-care, resilience, and empowerment. By making time for ourselves, we can reclaim our inner peace, nurture our spirits, and live lives that are truly aligned with our authentic selves.

Through the power of affirmations, we can reframe our mindset and cultivate a more resilient response to stress. Affirmations serve as reminders that we have the strength and capability to navigate challenging situations with grace and composure. They help us tap into our inner resources and remind us that we are in control of our emotions and reactions.

Within these pages, you will find a curated collection of affirmations designed to promote stress relief and relaxation. These affirmations will serve as gentle reminders to prioritize self-care and incorporate relaxation techniques into your daily routine. They will guide you toward moments of calm and tranquility, reminding you to take a step back, breathe deeply, and find solace in the present moment.

But affirmations alone are not enough. We will also provide you with practical tips and strategies for managing stress and integrating relaxation practices into your busy life. From mindfulness exercises to self-care rituals, you will discover a wealth of techniques that can help you find balance and restore your energy.

Stress relief and relaxation are not indulgences; they are essential components of a healthy and fulfilling life. By embracing these practices, you are not only investing in your own well-being but also setting an example for others. As busy Black women, we have the power to inspire and empower those around us, showing them that it is possible to prioritize self-care amid the demands of daily life.

So, as we embark on this journey of stress relief and relaxation, let us remember that we are deserving of moments of peace and rejuvenation. Through the power of affirmations and the adoption of healthy practices, we can cultivate a mindset that values our well-being and enables us to thrive. Together, let us create a new narrative of self-care, resilience, and self-empowerment for busy Black women everywhere.

Below are the top 10 empowering affirmations for stress relief and relaxation—embracing calm and inner peace:

1. "I release tension and embrace relaxation. I am worthy of rest and rejuvenation." – Oprah Winfrey
2. "I prioritize self-care as an essential part of my well-being. I deserve moments of peace and tranquility." – Michelle Obama

3. "I let go of stress and invite serenity into my life. I am in control of my emotions and choose to find calm in any situation." – Kamala Harris
4. "I create boundaries that protect my mental and emotional well-being. I choose to say no when it serves my self-care." – Serena Williams
5. "I honor my body's need for rest and replenishment. I embrace moments of stillness and allow myself to recharge." – Beyoncé
6. "I release the weight of stress and allow myself to unwind. I deserve moments of relaxation and self-care." – Ava DuVernay
7. "I prioritize my mental health and well-being. I engage in activities that bring me joy and peace of mind." – Viola Davis
8. "I release tension with every breath I take. I am deserving of a peaceful and stress-free life." – Misty Copeland
9. "I let go of worry and embrace tranquility. I find solace in moments of self-care and self-reflection." – Taraji P. Henson
10. "I am the master of my stress. I choose to focus on positive thoughts and invite peace into my life." – Issa Rae

NURTURING HEALTHY HABITS: EMBRACING A BALANCED AND VIBRANT LIFE

> *"Taking care of yourself is not selfish. It is essential. Nurturing healthy habits is the key to unlocking your full potential and living a life of vitality and fulfillment. Remember, you are worthy of the time and effort it takes to prioritize your well-being."*
>
> — BEYONCÉ

In this chapter, we delve into the importance of nurturing healthy habits as a foundation for overall well-being. As busy Black women, it is easy to get caught up in the demands of daily life and neglect our own health and self-care. However, by prioritizing and cultivating healthy habits, we can create a solid framework that supports both our physical and mental well-being.

SECTION 1: THE SIGNIFICANCE OF HEALTHY HABITS

Maintaining good health is a cornerstone of a fulfilling life. When we prioritize our well-being, we are better equipped to navigate the challenges and responsibilities that come our way. Healthy habits encompass a range of areas, including nutrition, exercise, sleep, and self-care. By consciously nurturing these habits, we can enhance our energy levels, boost our immune system, improve our mood, and foster a greater sense of self-care and self-love.

Below are the top 10 affirmations to maintain healthy habits:

1. I prioritize my health and well-being, knowing that by taking care of myself, I can better care for others.
2. I nourish my body with wholesome foods that energize and sustain me.
3. I engage in regular physical activity to strengthen my body and uplift my spirit.
4. I honor my need for rest and rejuvenation, ensuring that I get quality sleep each night.
5. I practice self-care as an act of self-love, recognizing that it is essential for my overall well-being.
6. I listen to my body's signals and give myself permission to rest when needed.
7. I cultivate a positive relationship with food, viewing it as fuel for my body and a source of nourishment.
8. I make time for relaxation and stress relief to promote balance and harmony in my life.

9. I create healthy boundaries that prioritize my well-being and prevent burnout.
10. I embrace the power of positive thinking, knowing that my mindset influences my overall health and happiness.

SECTION 2: AFFIRMATIONS FOR HEALTHY EATING

Our relationship with food plays a crucial role in our overall health. By incorporating affirmations that promote healthy eating into our daily routine, we can develop a positive mindset around food and make choices that nourish our bodies. These affirmations will inspire us to choose nutrient-rich foods, listen to the hunger and fullness cues of our bodies, and cultivate a healthy and balanced approach to eating:

1. I choose to fuel my body with wholesome and nutritious foods that support my health and well-being.
2. I honor my body's signals of hunger and fullness, eating mindfully and in tune with my body's needs.
3. I appreciate the abundance of fresh and natural foods available to me, and I make choices that align with my health goals.

4. I nourish my body with a variety of colorful fruits and vegetables, providing it with essential vitamins and minerals.
5. I prioritize whole grains and fiber-rich foods to support digestive health and sustained energy throughout the day.
6. I listen to my body's cravings with curiosity and make choices that balance indulgence with nourishment.
7. I savor each bite and eat with intention, fully enjoying the flavors and textures of my meals.
8. I choose water as my primary source of hydration, recognizing its importance in maintaining optimal health.
9. I release guilt and judgment around food, embracing a balanced and compassionate approach to nourishing myself.
10. I respect and appreciate my body, recognizing that it deserves to be nourished and cared for with love and respect.

SECTION 3: AFFIRMATIONS FOR EXERCISE AND MOVEMENT

Physical activity is vital for maintaining a strong and resilient body. The affirmations in this section will encourage us to embrace exercise and movement as an essential part of our self-care routine. They will motivate us to find joy in movement, explore different forms of exercise that we enjoy, and prioritize regular physical activity to keep our bodies strong and vibrant:

1. I love and appreciate my body, and I choose to honor it by engaging in regular physical activity.
2. I find joy in moving my body and discovering new ways to stay active.
3. I embrace exercise as an opportunity to nurture my physical and mental well-being.
4. I listen to my body's needs and engage in exercise that feels good and supports my overall health.

5. I celebrate my progress and achievements in my fitness journey, no matter how small they may seem.
6. I prioritize consistency in my exercise routine, knowing that small steps add up to significant results.
7. I am committed to challenging and pushing myself beyond my comfort zone to reach new levels of strength and fitness.
8. I create a supportive and encouraging environment for myself during workouts, celebrating my efforts and progress.
9. I appreciate the powerful connection between exercise and mental well-being, using movement as a tool to uplift my mood and reduce stress.
10. I am grateful for my body's capabilities and the opportunity to move and be active, and I make the most of it each day.

SECTION 4: AFFIRMATIONS FOR RESTFUL SLEEP

Quality sleep is essential for our physical and mental well-being. The affirmations in this section will help us cultivate a bedtime routine that promotes restful sleep and rejuvenation. They will guide us in creating a tranquil sleep environment, practicing relaxation techniques, and prioritizing adequate rest to wake up refreshed and ready to embrace each day:

1. I prioritize my sleep as a valuable investment in my overall well-being.
2. My bedroom is a sanctuary of peace and tranquility, promoting deep and restful sleep.
3. I release any tension or worries from the day, allowing my mind to quiet down for a peaceful night's sleep.
4. I create a consistent bedtime routine that signals to my body it's time to relax and unwind.
5. I practice relaxation techniques, such as deep breathing and progressive muscle relaxation, to prepare my body for restful sleep.
6. I let go of any thoughts or concerns that may keep me awake, knowing that tomorrow is a new day, and everything will work out.
7. I welcome peaceful and rejuvenating dreams that nourish my mind, body, and spirit.
8. I honor my need for sleep by setting boundaries and creating a sleep schedule that allows me to get the rest I need.

9. I choose to disconnect from electronic devices and stimulating activities before bed, creating a serene and calming environment.
10. I am grateful for the gift of sleep and the opportunity it gives me to recharge, restore, and wake up refreshed each morning.

SECTION 5: AFFIRMATIONS FOR SELF-CARE ROUTINES

Self-care is not a luxury; it is a necessity. The affirmations in this section will remind us to prioritize self-care as an essential part of our daily lives. They will encourage us to set boundaries, make time for activities that bring us joy and relaxation, and embrace self-care practices that nourish our mind, body, and soul:

1. I deserve to prioritize my own well-being and make self-care a nonnegotiable part of my daily routine.
2. I give myself permission to take breaks, recharge, and engage in activities that bring me joy and relaxation.
3. I honor my boundaries and say no to activities or commitments that drain my energy or overwhelm me.

4. I embrace self-care rituals that nourish my mind, body, and soul, knowing that they are essential for my overall well-being.
5. I listen to my inner needs and intuition, providing myself with the love and care I deserve.
6. I create a sacred space for self-reflection, meditation, or journaling to reconnect with myself on a deeper level.
7. I prioritize activities that bring me joy, whether it's reading a book, going for a walk in nature, or indulging in a creative outlet.
8. I engage in self-care practices that support my physical health, such as nourishing meals, regular exercise, and adequate rest.
9. I embrace moments of solitude and quiet to recharge and rejuvenate my spirit.
10. I celebrate and honor the journey of self-discovery and self-love, knowing that self-care is an act of empowerment and self-respect.

Nurturing healthy habits is a powerful act of self-love and self-preservation. By incorporating these affirmations into our daily routine, we are committing to our well-being and setting ourselves on a path toward a balanced and vibrant life. Let us embrace the power of healthy habits, cultivate self-care rituals, and honor ourselves as the strong, resilient, and deserving individuals that we are.

Remember, each small step we take toward nurturing healthy habits is a step toward a brighter and more fulfilling future. Together, let us embark on this journey of self-care and create a life that radiates vitality, joy, and well-being.

CULTIVATING POSITIVE THINKING

> "The greatest discovery of all time is that a person can change their future by merely changing their mindset. By cultivating positive thinking and embracing affirmations, we have the power to transform our lives and unlock the unlimited potential within us."
>
> — OPRAH WINFREY

In a world that can sometimes feel overwhelming, cultivating a positive mindset becomes an essential tool for navigating the challenges we encounter. It is through positive thinking that we can foster resilience, boost self-confidence, and create a life filled with joy and fulfillment. In this transformative chapter, we delve into the power of positive thinking and explore how daily affirmations can help us cultivate a mindset that empowers us to overcome obstacles and embrace the beauty of each moment.

Positive thinking is not about denying or ignoring the realities of life. It is about shifting our perspective and choosing to focus on the possibilities and solutions rather than dwelling on the problems. When we embrace positive thinking, we open ourselves up to a world of opportunities, growth, and happiness. It is a mindset that allows us to see setbacks as opportunities for growth, failures as stepping stones to success, and challenges as chances to learn and evolve.

Affirmations play a pivotal role in cultivating positive thinking. These powerful statements are a way of consciously choosing positive thoughts and beliefs that empower and uplift us. By repeating affirmations, we reprogram our subconscious mind, replacing negative self-talk with positive and empowering messages. As busy Black women, we often face unique challenges and societal pressures. Affirmations provide us with the tools to counteract negative narratives and embrace a mindset of self-belief, worthiness, and resilience.

In this chapter, we introduce a collection of affirmations specifically curated to foster positive thinking. These affirmations will guide us in challenging self-limiting beliefs, overcoming self-doubt, and embracing a mindset of abundance and possibility. They serve as gentle reminders to replace negative thoughts with positive ones, to reframe challenges as opportunities, and to cultivate gratitude and optimism in our daily lives.

To cultivate positive thinking, it is essential to develop strategies for reframing negative thoughts and fostering a positive outlook. One powerful technique is to practice mindfulness and awareness of our thoughts. By observing our thinking patterns, we can identify negative thought patterns and consciously choose to replace them with positive affirmations. This requires self-awareness and a commitment to self-reflection.

Another strategy is to surround ourselves with positivity. This can involve seeking out inspirational and uplifting content, such as books, podcasts, or online communities that promote positive thinking. Connecting with like-minded individuals who share our values and aspirations can also create a supportive and encouraging environment that reinforces positive thinking.

Gratitude is another powerful practice that cultivates a positive mindset. By focusing on the blessings and abundance in our lives, we shift our attention from lack to abundance, from problems to possibilities. Incorporating gratitude affirmations into our daily routine can help us appreciate the small moments of joy and find beauty in the simplest of things.

As we embark on this journey of cultivating positive thinking, it is important to remember that it is a practice. It requires consistency, patience, and self-compassion. We may stumble along the way, and that's okay. The key is to acknowledge our progress, celebrate our successes, and embrace the journey with an open heart and a resilient spirit.

By embracing positive thinking and incorporating affirmations into our daily lives, we have the power to transform our mindset and create a life filled with joy, purpose, and self-belief. Let us embark on this journey together, supporting and empowering one another to embrace positive thinking, cultivate resilience, and live our lives to the fullest.

In the words of Michelle Obama, "You have the power to change your mindset and create a positive and fulfilling life. Embrace the power of positive thinking and watch as it transforms your world."

1. I am worthy of love, success, and happiness. I embrace my worthiness and attract positive experiences into my life.

2. I choose to see challenges as opportunities for growth and learning. I am resilient and capable of overcoming any obstacles that come my way.
3. I release self-doubt and embrace self-confidence. I trust in my abilities and know that I am capable of achieving my goals.
4. I am in control of my thoughts and choose to focus on the positive. I replace negative thoughts with empowering and uplifting affirmations.
5. I am grateful for all that I have and all that is yet to come. I find joy in the present moment and appreciate the blessings in my life.
6. I believe in my own potential and know that I have the power to create the life I desire. I am the author of my own story.
7. I radiate positivity and attract positive people and experiences into my life. My positive energy uplifts and inspires those around me.
8. I embrace the power of optimism and approach each day with a positive mindset. I choose to see the good in every situation and trust in the unfolding of my journey.
9. I let go of fear and embrace courage. I step out of my comfort zone and take bold action toward my dreams and aspirations.

10. I am deserving of all the abundance and success that comes my way. I celebrate my achievements and welcome abundance into every area of my life.

These affirmations serve as reminders to cultivate positive thinking, challenge self-limiting beliefs, and embrace a mindset of abundance and possibility. By incorporating them into our daily lives, we empower ourselves to replace negative thoughts with positive ones, reframe challenges as opportunities, and cultivate gratitude and optimism.

SELF-CARE BEYOND THE DAILY AFFIRMATIONS

"Self-care is not a luxury; it's a necessity. We owe it to ourselves to prioritize our well-being, to practice self-reflection, and to seek the support we need. By embracing these practices, we empower ourselves to show up fully in all aspects of our lives."

— KAMALA HARRIS

In this chapter, we go beyond the daily affirmations and delve into additional self-care practices that can enhance our well-being and promote a deeper sense of self-nurturing. While the daily affirmations serve as a powerful tool for cultivating self-love, confidence, and empowerment, there are other practices that can further support our self-care journey. By exploring topics such as **self-reflection**, **self-compassion**, and **seeking support**, we can expand our self-care toolkit and create a comprehensive approach to nurturing our mind, body, and soul.

SECTION 1: THE POWER OF SELF-REFLECTION

The power of self-reflection is a practice that allows us to gain a deeper understanding of ourselves, our emotions, and our experiences. It provides an opportunity for introspection and self-discovery, allowing us to identify our needs, desires, and areas for growth. In this section, we explore various techniques for self-reflection, such as journaling, meditation, and mindfulness practices. We learn how to create sacred spaces for self-reflection, set intentions for our self-care journey, and gain clarity on our values and priorities.

Self-reflection is a transformative practice that holds the key to unlocking our true potential. It is a journey inward, where we navigate the depths of our being, exploring the intricate layers of our thoughts, emotions, and experiences. In this section, we embark on this sacred journey of self-discovery, guided by various techniques that invite us to engage in deep introspection and gain a profound understanding of ourselves.

One of the powerful tools we explore is journaling, a cathartic practice that allows us to pour our thoughts and emotions onto the pages of a notebook. Through the act of writing, we create a safe space to explore our inner landscape, uncovering hidden truths, and untangling the complexities of our minds. Whether it's a stream of conscious or guided prompts, journaling provides a therapeutic outlet for self-expression and reflection.

Meditation, another profound practice, invites us to still our minds and turn our attention inward. It is a moment of pause, where we can detach ourselves from the external noise and find solace in the present moment. Through mindfulness techniques, we cultivate a nonjudgmental awareness of our thoughts and emotions, allowing us to observe them without attachment or resistance. In this state of presence, we can gain clarity, develop self-awareness, and access our inner wisdom.

Creating sacred spaces for self-reflection is essential in fostering an environment conducive to deep introspection. Whether it's a cozy corner in our home, a peaceful outdoor spot, or a designated meditation space, these physical spaces serve as sanctuaries for us to retreat and connect with our inner selves. By intentionally setting up these spaces, we signal to ourselves the importance of self-reflection and provide ourselves with a nurturing environment to embark on this journey.

Setting intentions for our self-care journey is a powerful practice that allows us to align our actions with our values and aspirations. By clarifying what we seek to achieve through self-reflection, we create a roadmap that guides our path. These intentions can be simple yet profound, such as seeking self-acceptance, cultivating inner peace, or fostering personal growth. They serve as guiding stars, reminding us of our purpose and driving us forward on our self-care journey.

Ultimately, self-reflection empowers us to gain clarity on our values and priorities. By delving deep within ourselves, we uncover what truly matters to us, what brings us joy and fulfillment, and what ignites our passion. Armed with this knowledge, we can make conscious choices that align with our authentic selves and lead us toward a more purposeful and meaningful life.

In the world of self-care, self-reflection is a transformative practice that allows us to uncover the depths of our being, gain profound insights, and chart our course toward personal growth and fulfillment. Through journaling, meditation, creating sacred spaces, and setting intentions, we open the door to self-discovery and embark on a journey that brings us closer to our true selves. Let us embrace the power of self-reflection and embark on this transformative path of self-discovery.

SECTION 2: CULTIVATING SELF-COMPASSION

Self-compassion is a vital component of self-care, as it involves treating ourselves with kindness, understanding, and acceptance. In this section, we delve into the practice of self-compassion and learn how to cultivate a compassionate mindset toward ourselves. We explore techniques for self-soothing, practicing self-acceptance, and embracing imperfections. By developing self-compassion, we create a nurturing and supportive inner environment that fosters our overall well-being.

Self-compassion is a gentle embrace of our own humanity, a practice that allows us to extend kindness, understanding, and acceptance to ourselves. It is a crucial element of self-care, for it recognizes that we, too, are deserving of love and compassion. In this section, we embark on a journey of cultivating self-compassion, learning how to be our own greatest ally and champion.

One of the key aspects of cultivating self-compassion is the practice of self-soothing. When we encounter moments of stress, self-doubt, or pain, we can turn inward and offer ourselves comfort and support. Just as we would console a dear friend, we can gently remind ourselves that it is okay to struggle, that it is a natural part of the human experience. Through self-soothing techniques such as deep breathing, soothing affirmations, or engaging in activities that bring us joy, we nurture our souls and provide ourselves with the care and tenderness we deserve.

Practicing self-acceptance is another essential component of cultivating self-compassion. It involves embracing all aspects of ourselves, including our flaws, mistakes, and imperfections. Rather than striving for perfection, we learn to appreciate our unique qualities and acknowledge that growth comes from embracing our vulnerabilities. By letting go of self-judgment and embracing self-acceptance, we create a nurturing inner environment where we can truly flourish.

In our journey toward self-compassion, we must also embrace the idea that imperfections are not shortcomings but opportunities for growth and learning. Instead of berating ourselves for our mistakes, we can reframe them as valuable lessons and stepping stones toward personal growth. By embracing imperfections, we release the burden of unrealistic expectations and allow ourselves the freedom to explore, experiment, and evolve.

Cultivating self-compassion requires us to practice self-care in all aspects of our lives. It means setting boundaries, prioritizing our needs, and recognizing when we need to replenish our own well-being. It means speaking to ourselves with kindness and offering ourselves grace during times of difficulty. By treating ourselves with the same compassion and understanding we extend to others, we create a nurturing and supportive inner environment that fosters our overall well-being.

In a world that often encourages self-criticism and unrealistic standards, self-compassion becomes an act of rebellion. It is a radical act of self-love that challenges societal norms and allows us to honor our authentic selves. As we cultivate self-compassion, we not only transform our relationship with ourselves but also become beacons of compassion and empathy for others.

Let us embark on this journey of self-compassion, recognizing that it is through kindness and acceptance toward ourselves that we can truly thrive. By embracing self-soothing techniques, practicing self-acceptance, and embracing imperfections, we create a foundation of self-compassion that supports our well-being and empowers us to live authentically and wholeheartedly. Together, let us nurture a culture of self-compassion and extend its ripple effect to the world around us.

SECTION 3: SEEKING SUPPORT AND CONNECTION

Self-care is not meant to be a solitary journey. Seeking support and connection with others can greatly enhance our self-care practices. In this section, we explore the importance of building a support network and seeking out relationships that uplift and empower us. We discuss the benefits of therapy, coaching, and mentorship, as well as the value of community and support groups. By connecting with others who share similar experiences and goals, we create a sense of belonging and find solace in knowing that we are not alone on our self-care journey.

Self-care is a transformative journey that becomes even more powerful when we invite others to walk alongside us. It is through seeking support and connection that we can truly thrive and navigate the challenges and triumphs of life. In this section, we delve into the significance of building a support network and actively seeking relationships that uplift and empower us.

One of the most impactful ways to enhance our self-care practices is by seeking professional support. Therapy, coaching, and mentorship provide invaluable guidance and insight as we navigate our personal growth and well-being. These avenues of support offer a safe space for us to explore our thoughts, emotions, and experiences, providing us with tools and strategies to overcome challenges and embrace our authentic selves. Through the guidance of these professionals, we can gain a deeper understanding of ourselves, uncover hidden strengths, and tap into our true potential.

In addition to professional support, the power of community and connection cannot be overstated. Building relationships with individuals who share similar experiences, aspirations, and goals can be immensely empowering. Engaging in support groups, whether in person or online, creates a sense of belonging and allows us to find solace in knowing that we are not alone on our self-care journey. Within these communities, we can share our challenges, celebrate our victories, and learn from the collective wisdom and experiences of others.

By actively seeking support and connection, we create a network of individuals who uplift, inspire, and challenge us to become the best versions of ourselves. These relationships serve as mirrors, reflecting our strengths and reminding us of our inherent worth. They provide encouragement, accountability, and a space for us to celebrate our progress and growth. Through the power of connection, we realize that self-care is not a solitary endeavor but a collective journey toward personal fulfillment and well-being.

It is important to remember that seeking support is not a sign of weakness but rather a testament to our strength and commitment to our own well-being. By acknowledging that we can benefit from the wisdom and support of others, we demonstrate a deep sense of self-awareness and humility. We open ourselves up to new perspectives, insights, and opportunities for growth.

As we embrace the power of seeking support and connection, we contribute to a culture of collective care and empowerment. We become not only recipients of support but also sources of inspiration and encouragement for others. Together, we create a web of resilience, compassion, and understanding that transcends individual boundaries and empowers us to live authentically and wholeheartedly.

Let us cherish the power of seeking support and connection, recognizing that our journeys are made richer and more meaningful when we share them with others. Through the relationships we cultivate, the professional support we seek, and the communities we engage with, we create a tapestry of support that uplifts and empowers us. Together, let us nurture a culture of connection and support, where self-care is celebrated as a collective endeavor, and no one journeys alone.

SECTION 4: EXPLORING SELF-CARE RESOURCES

In this final section, we provide recommendations and resources for further exploration of self-care practices. We share books, podcasts, websites, and other tools that can deepen our understanding of self-care and provide guidance and inspiration along the way. We encourage readers to continue their self-care journey beyond the book, embracing a lifelong commitment to nurturing their well-being.

Books serve as portals to new ideas, perspectives, and insights. They have the power to inspire, educate, and empower us on our self-care journey. We recommend exploring a range of self-care books that resonate with your interests and needs. Whether you are seeking practical strategies, personal narratives, or expert guidance, there is a book out there that can provide the wisdom and support you are looking for. Some notable titles to consider include *365 Days of Daily Affirmations for Black Women* by Michelle Woods, *The Self-Care Solution* by Jennifer Ashton, *Radical Self-Care for Black Women* by Jonnae Thompson, and *The Gifts of Imperfection* by Brené Brown.

Podcasts have become a popular medium for self-care enthusiasts to access information, stories, and conversations about well-being. These audio platforms offer a wealth of content that can inspire, uplift, and educate. Consider subscribing to podcasts that focus on self-care, mindfulness, personal growth, and empowerment. Some noteworthy podcasts include *The Lavendaire Lifestyle* hosted by Aileen Xu, *Black Girl in Om* hosted by Lauren Ash and Deun Ivory, and *The Self-Care Sunday Podcast* hosted by Kayley Reed.

Websites and online platforms provide a treasure trove of resources for self-care. From blogs to online communities, there is a wealth of information waiting to be explored. Seek out websites that align with your interests and values, offering articles, courses, and tools to support your self-care journey. Some notable websites include *Tiny Buddha*, *The Nap Ministry*, and *The Blissful Mind*. These platforms offer a wealth of articles, guides, and resources that can enhance your understanding of self-care and provide practical tips for implementation.

Social media has also emerged as a powerful tool for self-care inspiration and community building. Follow accounts and hashtags that promote self-care, mindfulness, and personal growth. Engage with content that resonates with you and participate in conversations that encourage self-reflection and connection. Social media platforms can be a source of daily inspiration and reminders to prioritize your well-being.

In addition to these resources, consider seeking out workshops, retreats, and classes that align with your self-care goals. These immersive experiences offer opportunities to deepen your practice, learn from experts, and connect with like-minded individuals. Explore local offerings in your area or consider attending virtual events that cater to your specific interests.

As we conclude this book, remember that self-care is a lifelong journey. It is a commitment to prioritize your well-being and cultivate practices that nourish your mind, body, and soul. Embrace the resources available to you, and continue to explore, learn, and grow. Let self-care be a constant presence in your life, reminding you of your worth, resilience, and the power you hold within.

In the spirit of collective care and empowerment, share your discoveries and recommendations with others. As you uncover valuable resources, pass them along to friends, family, and community members who can benefit from them. Together, we can create a culture of self-care that uplifts and empowers us all.

Remember, your self-care journey is unique to you. Explore, experiment, and find what resonates with your needs and desires. Embrace the power of self-care resources as tools to support and enhance your well-being. And as you continue on this transformative path, know that you are not alone. We are a community of busy Black women, supporting and uplifting one another as we navigate the complexities of life with grace and resilience.

Conclusion: In the journey of self-care, daily affirmations are just the beginning. Chapter 7 explores additional self-care practices that complement the affirmations and foster a holistic approach to self-nurturing. By engaging in self-reflection, cultivating self-compassion, and seeking support and connection, we expand our self-care toolkit and create a strong foundation for personal growth and well-being. Let us continue to prioritize our self-care journey, embracing these practices and exploring the resources available to us. Together, we can create a culture of self-care that uplifts and empowers busy Black women everywhere.

CONCLUSION: EMBRACING THE POWER OF SELF-CARE

"Self-care is not selfish or self-indulgent. It is simply giving the world the best of you, instead of what's left of you."

— MICHELLE OBAMA

90 | CONCLUSION: EMBRACING THE POWER OF SELF-CARE

As we come to the end of our transformative journey through *Daily Self-Care Affirmations for Busy Black Women: Cultivating Self-Care Habits; Empowering Practices for a Healthy Mind, Body, and Soul*, it is essential to reflect on the key takeaways and the profound impact that self-care can have on our lives. We have explored various aspects of self-care, from mindfulness and stress relief to healthy habits and positive thinking.

CONCLUSION: EMBRACING THE POWER OF SELF-CARE

Throughout this book, we have emphasized the importance of prioritizing our well-being and nurturing ourselves amid our busy lives.

One of the fundamental lessons we have learned is that self-care is not a luxury or an indulgence; it is a necessity. As busy Black women, we often find ourselves juggling multiple responsibilities and wearing many hats. It is easy to lose sight of our own needs and put our well-being on the back burner. However, we must recognize that taking care of ourselves is not selfish—it is an act of self-love and empowerment.

Daily affirmations have emerged as a powerful tool for cultivating a positive mindset and nurturing our overall well-being. By incorporating affirmations into our daily routines, we have the opportunity to rewire our brains, challenge self-limiting beliefs, and embrace a mindset of possibility and abundance. The affirmations shared in this book have been carefully curated to resonate with the experiences and aspirations of busy Black women. They serve as gentle reminders to love ourselves, honor our boundaries, and prioritize self-care as an integral part of our lives.

Throughout our journey, we have explored the science behind self-care and the profound impact it can have on our mental, emotional, and physical health. Research has shown that self-care practices such as mindfulness, healthy habits, and positive thinking can reduce stress, enhance resilience, and improve overall well-being. By incorporating these practices into our lives, we empower ourselves to navigate the challenges we face with grace, embrace our authentic selves, and thrive in all aspects of life.

As we conclude this book, I urge you, my fellow busy Black women, to commit to incorporating daily affirmations and self-care practices into your lives. Embrace the power that lies within you to prioritize your well-being, no matter how demanding your schedule may be. Start small and be consistent. Find moments of stillness and quiet amid the chaos. Make self-care nonnegotiable—just as you do with your other commitments.

Remember that self-care is a lifelong journey. It is not about achieving perfection or adhering to a rigid set of rules. It is about listening to your needs, honoring your boundaries, and embracing practices that nourish your mind, body, and soul. Allow yourself the grace to evolve, grow, and adapt your self-care practices as you navigate different seasons of life.

Lastly, I encourage you to share the wisdom and insights you have gained from this book with other busy Black women in your life. Spark conversations, create a community of support, and uplift one another on this self-care journey. Together, we can shatter the notion that self-care is a luxury reserved for a select few. We can redefine self-care as a radical act of self-love and resilience that is accessible to all.

I am confident that by embracing daily affirmations and self-care practices, you will experience a profound transformation in your life. Your mental and emotional well-being will flourish, your relationships will deepen, and your ability to navigate challenges will be strengthened. You are worthy of the love, care, and attention you give to others, and it is time to extend that same love and care to yourself.

As you close this book, carry the lessons and insights with you as a guiding light. Let self-care be the foundation upon which you build a life filled with joy, fulfillment, and purpose. Embrace the power within you to nurture yourself, for when you are at your best, you have the strength to uplift and empower those around you.

With love and gratitude,
Michelle Woods

SUMMARY

Repeating daily affirmations offers a multitude of benefits that can transform our lives as busy Black women. By engaging in the practice of positive self-talk, we cultivate a mindset rooted in self-belief, resilience, and empowerment. Affirmations serve as powerful reminders of our worth and potential, enabling us to overcome self-doubt, embrace our unique strengths, and navigate life's challenges with confidence and grace. Through the repetition of affirmations, we rewire our minds, replacing negative thoughts and limiting beliefs with empowering and uplifting narratives. This practice not only boosts our self-esteem but also enhances our overall well-being, fostering a positive outlook, reducing stress, and increasing our ability to manifest our dreams and aspirations. By investing time in daily affirmations, we unlock our inner power and unleash our true potential, paving the way for personal growth, success, and a life filled with purpose and fulfillment.

60 Powerful Daily Affirmations for Self-Care Routines

1. I am deserving of love, care, and respect.
2. My well-being is a priority, and I honor it every day.
3. I choose to prioritize self-care as an essential part of my life.
4. I am worthy of taking time for myself and nurturing my needs.
5. I release all feelings of guilt and embrace self-care without reservation.
6. I am resilient and capable of overcoming any challenges that come my way.
7. I am in control of my own happiness and well-being.
8. I embrace self-compassion and treat myself with kindness and understanding.
9. I nourish my body with healthy choices and listen to its needs.
10. I am grateful for the opportunity to care for myself and show love to myself.
11. I release all negative thoughts and replace them with positive affirmations.
12. I trust in my abilities and believe in my own potential.
13. I am deserving of rest and rejuvenation, and I prioritize quality sleep.

14. I am mindful of my thoughts, words, and actions, and I choose positivity.
15. I am worthy of setting boundaries that protect my mental and emotional well-being.
16. I release all self-doubt and embrace my unique strengths and talents.
17. I choose to let go of what no longer serves me and make space for growth.
18. I am worthy of forgiveness, both for myself and for others.
19. I honor my emotions and give myself permission to feel and express them.
20. I am surrounded by love and support, and I attract positive relationships.
21. I am capable of achieving my goals and creating the life I desire.
22. I am worthy of pursuing my passions and embracing my creative side.
23. I prioritize activities that bring me joy and nourish my soul.
24. I am enough, just as I am, and I embrace my uniqueness.
25. I let go of perfectionism and embrace progress and growth.
26. I am capable of handling any challenges that come my way.

27. I am deserving of love, success, and abundance in all areas of my life.
28. I radiate confidence and embrace my own worthiness.
29. I release all comparisons and focus on my own journey and progress.
30. I am grateful for the small moments of joy and beauty in my daily life.
31. I practice gratitude and appreciate the blessings that surround me.
32. I release all self-criticism and embrace self-acceptance and self-love.
33. I am an important and valuable part of this world.
34. I trust in the process of life and know that everything unfolds as it should.
35. I am in tune with my intuition and trust its guidance.
36. I choose to let go of past hurts and create a future filled with joy and peace.
37. I am open to new possibilities and opportunities for growth and learning.
38. I attract positivity and abundance into my life.
39. I am present in the moment and fully embrace the here and now.
40. I honor my boundaries and say no to things that drain my energy.

41. I am worthy of self-care rituals that bring me relaxation and rejuvenation.
42. I celebrate my achievements, no matter how small, and acknowledge my progress.
43. I am committed to my personal growth and investing time in self-improvement.
44. I choose thoughts that uplift and inspire me, and I let go of negativity.
45. I am resilient and bounce back from setbacks with grace and determination.
46. I nourish my mind with positive and empowering information.
47. I release all fears and step out of my comfort zone to pursue my dreams.
48. I am deserving of self-care rituals that bring me peace and serenity.
49. I listen to my body's needs and provide my body with nourishment and movement.
50. I choose to surround myself with people who support and uplift me.
51. I release all self-imposed limitations and embrace my limitless potential.
52. I am the creator of my own happiness and joy.
53. I attract abundance and prosperity into my life.
54. I let go of negative self-talk and replace it with words of encouragement and empowerment.

55. I am grateful for the lessons that challenges bring, as they contribute to my growth.
56. I release all doubts about my abilities and trust in my innate strength and resilience.
57. I am open to receiving love, support, and kindness from others.
58. I choose to forgive myself and others, freeing myself from the burden of resentment.
59. I am deserving of a life filled with love, joy, and fulfillment.
60. I embrace solitude and find strength in moments of quiet reflection.

These affirmations are designed to uplift and empower you on your self-care journey. Repeat them daily and allow their positive energy to guide you toward a life of self-love and well-being. Remember, you are worthy of taking care of yourself and embracing the beauty of your own existence.

60 Powerful Daily Affirmations to Maintain Healthy Habits

1. I prioritize my health and well-being above all else.
2. I nourish my body with wholesome and nutritious foods.
3. I am committed to regular exercise and staying physically active.
4. I listen to my body's needs and give it the rest it deserves.
5. I release all negative thoughts and embrace a positive mindset.
6. I am in control of my choices and make healthy decisions each day.
7. I honor my body and treat it with love and respect.
8. I am grateful for the opportunity to care for my physical and mental health.
9. I am committed to maintaining a balanced and healthy lifestyle.
10. I find joy in staying hydrated and nourishing my body with water.
11. I choose to prioritize sleep as an essential part of my well-being.
12. I am mindful of the portion sizes I consume and eat in moderation.

13. I am dedicated to incorporating fruits and vegetables into my daily meals.
14. I find pleasure in preparing and cooking healthy meals for myself.
15. I embrace the power of mindful eating and savor each bite.
16. I am in tune with my body's hunger and fullness cues.
17. I am committed to reducing my intake of processed and sugary foods.
18. I make time for regular physical activity that brings me joy.
19. I challenge myself to try new forms of exercise and embrace variety.
20. I find motivation and inspiration in the progress I see in my fitness journey.
21. I am proud of my body and appreciate all that it can do.
22. I am grateful for my body's strength and resilience.
23. I create a supportive environment that encourages healthy habits.
24. I surround myself with like-minded individuals who uplift and inspire me.
25. I find balance in indulging in occasional treats without guilt.

26. I release all negative associations with food and embrace a positive relationship.
27. I am mindful of my eating habits even during social gatherings and celebrations.
28. I nourish my body with whole foods that provide energy and vitality.
29. I take breaks throughout the day to stretch and move my body.
30. I prioritize self-care and make time for activities that bring me joy and relaxation.
31. I find peace in practicing meditation and connecting with my inner self.
32. I embrace self-discipline and make choices that align with my health goals.
33. I am resilient and capable of overcoming any challenges that come my way.
34. I choose to see setbacks as opportunities for growth and learning.
35. I am committed to making long-term changes that support my health and well-being.
36. I am grateful for my body's ability to heal and regenerate.
37. I prioritize self-care rituals that nourish my mind, body, and soul.
38. I am dedicated to practicing gratitude for my health and vitality.

39. I release all comparisons and embrace my own unique journey to health.
40. I am patient with myself and celebrate every small step toward my goals.
41. I listen to my body's signals and respond with love and compassion.
42. I create a peaceful environment that promotes relaxation and stress reduction.
43. I am aware of the impact of stress on my health and actively manage it.
44. I find solace in activities that bring me peace and tranquility.
45. I embrace moments of stillness and allow my mind to rest and rejuvenate.
46. I practice deep breathing to calm my mind and bring clarity to my thoughts.
47. I choose to let go of things that no longer serve my well-being.
48. I trust in the process of my journey to a healthier and happier life.
49. I am resilient and can overcome any obstacles that come my way.
50. I honor and respect my body's need for movement.
51. I release all tension and stress from my body, allowing it to relax and unwind.

52. I am in tune with my body's signals and provide it with the care it deserves.
53. I embrace the power of positive affirmations to uplift and motivate myself.
54. I attract and manifest vibrant health and well-being into my life.
55. I am deserving of optimal health and vitality.
56. I am committed to taking consistent steps toward my health goals.
57. I trust my intuition in making choices that support my well-being.
58. I nourish my mind with positive thoughts and empowering beliefs.
59. I am grateful for the opportunity to prioritize my health and well-being.
60. I radiate with vibrant energy and vitality, embracing a life of optimal health.

Remember, each affirmation holds the power to transform your mindset and support you on your journey toward maintaining healthy habits. Embrace these affirmations daily, allowing them to guide and uplift you as you prioritize your health and well-being.

60 Power Affirmations for Mindfulness, Stress Relief, and Positive Thinking

20 Affirmations for Mindfulness:

1. I am fully present in this moment, embracing the beauty and possibilities it holds.
2. I anchor my attention to the present, letting go of worries about the past or future.
3. I cultivate a calm and centered mind, free from judgment and attachment.
4. I embrace each experience with curiosity and openness, allowing it to unfold naturally.
5. I connect deeply with my breath, using it as a guide to stay grounded and present.
6. I observe my thoughts and emotions with kindness and compassion, without getting swept away by them.
7. I find stillness and peace within, even amid the chaos of daily life.
8. I appreciate the simple joys and beauty that surround me in each moment.
9. I let go of expectations and surrender to the flow of life.
10. I engage in activities mindfully, savoring every sensation, and fully immersing myself in the present moment.

11. I approach challenges with resilience and a calm mind, knowing that I have the inner strength to overcome them.
12. I practice gratitude for the abundance that exists in my life, big and small.
13. I release stress and tension from my body and mind, allowing relaxation to wash over me.
14. I find moments of peace and tranquility amid a busy day.
15. I let go of what I cannot control and focus on what I can influence in the present moment.
16. I prioritize self-care and make time for activities that nourish my soul and replenish my energy.
17. I create space for silence and stillness, allowing my intuition to guide me.
18. I connect with the natural world, finding solace and inspiration in its beauty.
19. I practice self-compassion, treating myself with kindness and understanding in all moments.
20. I am a witness to my own experiences, fully embracing the present and finding meaning in each moment.

20 Affirmations for Stress Relief:

1. I release stress and tension from my body and mind, allowing peace to flow through me.
2. I choose to focus on the present moment, letting go of worries about the future.
3. I trust in my ability to handle any challenges that come my way.
4. I find calmness in the midst of chaos, maintaining a centered and grounded state of mind.
5. I prioritize self-care and create boundaries to protect my well-being.
6. I give myself permission to rest and recharge when needed.
7. I let go of what is beyond my control, freeing myself from unnecessary stress.
8. I engage in activities that bring me joy and relaxation, replenishing my energy.
9. I practice deep breathing to calm my mind and release tension from my body.
10. I seek support and reach out to loved ones when I need assistance or a listening ear.
11. I embrace a positive mindset, choosing to focus on gratitude and optimism.
12. I find moments of laughter and joy, allowing them to uplift my spirit.

13. I nurture myself with nourishing foods and engage in regular physical activity to reduce stress.
14. I engage in hobbies and activities that bring me a sense of peace and fulfillment.
15. I set healthy boundaries with work and commitments, allowing myself time for relaxation and self-care.
16. I practice mindfulness and stay present, avoiding unnecessary worries and distractions.
17. I let go of perfectionism and embrace the beauty of imperfection.
18. I take breaks throughout the day to pause, breathe, and reset my mind and body.
19. I detach from negative thoughts and replace them with positive affirmations and empowering beliefs.
20. I am in control of my response to stress, choosing calmness and resilience in the face of challenges.

20 Affirmations for Positive Thinking:

1. I choose to see the beauty and potential in every situation.
2. I am worthy of love, success, and happiness.
3. I believe in my abilities and trust in my own inner wisdom.
4. I attract positivity and abundance into my life.
5. I am surrounded by love, support, and positivity.
6. I let go of self-limiting beliefs and embrace a mindset of growth and possibility.
7. I am grateful for the blessings and opportunities that come my way.
8. I celebrate my achievements and acknowledge my strengths.
9. I radiate positivity and uplift others with my words and actions.
10. I am resilient and capable of overcoming any obstacles.
11. I choose thoughts that empower and inspire me.
12. I am the author of my own story, and I create a narrative of success and happiness.
13. I am deserving of all the good things life has to offer.

14. I embrace optimism and find the silver lining in every situation.
15. I am open to receiving and manifesting my dreams and desires.
16. I attract positive relationships that uplift and support me.
17. I release negative thoughts and replace them with positive affirmations.
18. I am in control of my thoughts, and I choose to focus on what serves my highest good.
19. I approach challenges as opportunities for growth and learning.
20. I am a beacon of positivity and light, inspiring others with my optimistic outlook.

Remember, each day is an opportunity to embrace mindfulness, find stress relief, and cultivate positive thinking. By integrating these powerful affirmations into your daily routine, you can foster a mindset of self-care, resilience, and joy. Embrace the power of positive affirmations and watch as your life transforms in beautiful and empowering ways.

LET'S INSPIRE AND EMPOWER OTHER WOMEN

Congratulations on embarking on your journey towards self-love, confidence, and empowerment through "Daily Self-Care Affirmations for Busy Black Women: Cultivating Self-Care Habits; Empowering Practices for a Healthy Mind, Body, and Soul." You've taken bold steps to cultivate a positive mindset and embrace your true worth. Now, let's extend our support and help other women light their path to personal growth and transformation.

> *"There is no limit to what we, as women, can accomplish."*
>
> — MICHELLE OBAMA

By sharing your honest opinion of this book on Amazon, you have the incredible opportunity to guide other women on their own empowering journey. Your review will serve as a guiding light, helping them discover the transformative power of daily affirmations and the positive impact it can have on their lives.

We understand the significance of cultivating self-care habits and empowering practices for a healthy mind, body, and soul. Together, we can break barriers and empower busy black women to prioritize their well-being and embrace daily self-care affirmations. By leaving a review, you contribute to a collective effort to inspire and guide others toward nurturing self-care routines that fuel their inner strength and radiate unwavering confidence. Let's create a community of empowered women who uplift and support one another on their journey toward self-love and holistic well-being.

MAKE A LASTING IMPRESSION!

Your support in leaving an honest review on Amazon is invaluable. It provides a roadmap for women seeking guidance, ensuring they find the inspiration and resources necessary to embark on their own empowering transformation. Your words have the power to ignite confidence, spark hope, and propel others towards financial freedom.

We appreciate your commitment to supporting and uplifting women. By sharing your experience and insights, you contribute to a powerful community of women who come together to inspire, motivate, and empower one another.

Scan the QR code below to leave a quick review on Amazon. Your voice matters, and together we can create a brighter future for women seeking personal and financial growth.

Thank you for being a beacon of light on this transformative journey. Together, let's illuminate the path for other women, empowering them to embrace their inner strength and radiate unwavering confidence.

IMAGE RESOURCES

Geralt. (2017, June 23). *Board School Self Confidence - Free photo on Pixabay*. Pixabay. https://pixabay.com/photos/board-school-self-confidence-2433978/

Janeb. (2016, January 8). *Michelle Obama Official Portrait - Free photo on Pixabay*. Pixabay. https://pixabay.com/photos/michelle-obama-official-portrait-1129160/

Oyebolaolugbemi. (2020, December 12). *Window Quote Motivation - Free photo on Pixabay*. Pixabay. https://pixabay.com/photos/window-quote-motivation-5822196/

Anilsharma. (2022, April 19). *Yoga Class Pose - Free photo on Pixabay*. Pixabay. https://pixabay.com/photos/yoga-yoga-class-yoga-pose-7140566/

IqbalStock. (2021, December 22). *Self Care Writing Note - Free photo on Pixabay*. Pixabay. https://pixabay.com/photos/self-care-writing-note-morning-6886588/

Activedia. (2019, October 16). *Spiritualism Awakening Meditation - Free photo on Pixabay*. Pixabay. https://pixabay.com/photos/spiritualism-awakening-meditation-4552237/

Tinytribes. (2020, January 20). *Self-Care Health Relax - Free photo on Pixabay*. Pixabay. https://pixabay.com/photos/self-care-health-relax-self-4778282/

Palinska. (2020, April 29). *Tree Park Nature - Free photo on Pixabay*. Pixabay. https://pixabay.com/photos/tree-park-nature-forest-landscape-5102896/

Trevoykellyphotography. (2018, January 25). *People Three Portrait - Free photo on Pixabay*. Pixabay. https://pixabay.com/photos/people-three-portrait-black-3104635/

Made in the USA
Columbia, SC
02 February 2025